The Fish Thief

By Jenny Moore

Illustrated by
Ramona Bruno

It was Inspector Parkin's birthday.

X102230

The item should be returned or renewed
by the last date stamped below.

Dylid dychwelyd neu adnewyddu'r eitem erbyn
y dyddiad olaf sydd wedi'i stampio isod.

Newport
CITY COUNCIL
CYNGOR DINAS
Casnewydd

PILLGWENLLY

To renew visit / Adnewyddwch ar
www.newport.gov.uk/libraries

Maverick
Early Readers

'The Fish Thief'
An original concept by Jenny Moore
© Jenny Moore 2024

Illustrated by Ramona Bruno

Published by MAVERICK ARTS PUBLISHING LTD
Studio 11, City Business Centre, 6 Brighton Road,
Horsham, West Sussex, RH13 5BB
© Maverick Arts Publishing Limited May 2024
+44 (0)1403 256941

A CIP catalogue record for this book is available at the British Library.

ISBN 978-1-83511-002-7

Printed in India

www.maverickbooks.co.uk

Green

This book is rated as: Green Band (Guided Reading)
It follows the requirements for Phase 5 phonics.
Most words are decodable, and any non-decodable words are familiar,
supported by the context and/or represented in the artwork.

Thank you for the fish.
I will enjoy eating it.

From Fish Fingers Fred,
the fearless fish thief.

"We'll see about that,"

muttered Inspector Parkin.

"Nobody steals my fish and
gets away with it."

He spotted a trail of wet footprints
leading outside.

"The prints must belong to
Fish Fingers Fred! I'll follow them
and catch him red-handed."

Inspector Parkin set off into the snow to find his missing fish.

He followed the trail of prints

all the way into town.

He kept a sharp lookout for Fred as he went, but there was no sign of him.

The streets were empty.

"That's strange," he murmured.

The trail of prints stopped outside

the Fishy Flipper Bar.

Inspector Parkin sniffed the air.

"I smell fish," he muttered. "My fish."

"I've got you now, Fish Fingers Fred!"

he shouted.

He swung open the door and

looked about him in shock.

The Fishy Flipper Bar was empty too.

Where was Fish Fingers Fred?

Where was his missing birthday fish?

Was he too late?

Inspector Parkin jumped.

The Fishy Flipper Bar wasn't empty at all!

"Happy Birthday, Inspector Parkin!"

Inspector Parkin grinned.

"Thank you!" he said.

"Birthday fish for one is nice.

But birthday fish to share is

much better!"

Quiz

1. What is Inspector Parkin planning to eat for his birthday dinner?
a) A cake
b) A nice big fish
c) A pie

2. Who does Inspector Parkin think has stolen his fish?
a) Fish Fingers Fred
b) Fish Fingers Frank
c) Fish Fingers Fran

3. What does Inspector Parkin follow?
a) A trail of footprints
b) A trail of crumbs
c) A trail of feathers

4. Where does the trail stop?

a) Inspector Parkin's house

b) The Penguin Café

c) The Fishy Flipper Bar

5. Who is in the bar at the end?

a) No one

b) Fish Fingers Fred

c) Inspector Parkin's friends

26/7/24

Book Bands for Guided Reading

The Institute of Education book banding system is a scale of colours that reflects the various levels of reading difficulty. The bands are assigned by taking into account the content, the language style, the layout and phonics. Word, phrase and sentence level work is also taken into consideration.

Maverick Early Readers are a bright, attractive range of books covering the pink to white bands. All of these books have been book banded for guided reading to the industry standard and edited by a leading educational consultant.

To view the whole Maverick Readers scheme, visit our website at www.maverickearlyreaders.com

Or scan the QR code above to view our scheme instantly!

Quiz Answers: 1b, 2a, 3a, 4c, 5c

Pink
Red
Yellow
Blue
Green
Orange
Turquoise
Purple
Gold
White